SUBWAY LINE, No. 13

Philosophical Thinking is Yoga for the Mind®

Upper West Side Philosophers, Inc. provides a
publication venue for original philosophical
thinking steeped in lived life, in line with our
motto: *philosophical living & lived philosophy.*

Lev Petrovich Yakubinsky

ON LANGUAGE & POETRY

Three Essays

*Translated from the Russian, edited and
with an Introduction by Michael Eskin*

Upper West Side Philosophers, Inc.
New York · 2018

Published by Upper West Side Philosophers, Inc.
P. O. Box 250645, New York, NY 10025, USA
www.westside-philosophers.com /
www.yogaforthemind.us

English translation copyright © 2018 by Upper West Side
Philosophers, Inc.

Yoga for the Mind[R]

The colophon is a registered trademark of Upper West Side
Philosophers, Inc.

Library of Congress Cataloging-in-Publication Data

Names: Yakubinsky, Lev Petrovich, 1892-1945 author. | Eskin,
Michael
  translator editor.
Title: On language & poetry : three essays / Lev Petrovich Yakubinsky ; translated from the Russian, edited, and with an introduction by Michael Eskin.
Other titles: On language and poetry
Description: New York : Upper West Side Philosophers, Inc., |
Series: Subway line ; no. 13 | Includes index.
Identifiers: LCCN 2017015857 | ISBN 9781935830511 (pbk. :
alk. paper)
Subjects: LCSH: Poetics. | Language and languages--Philosophy.
  | Saussure, Ferdinand de, 1857-1913--Criticism and
  interpretation.
Classification: LCC PN1042 .Y35 2017 | DDC 808.1--dc23
LC record available at https://lccn.loc.gov/2017015857

CONTENTS

Introduction
The Forgotten Formalist

Even among the cognoscenti—linguists, literary critics, and cultural theorists—the name 'Yakubinsky' will not necessarily ring a bell. But it should: for his significance for modern poetics and criticism can hardly be overestimated. Occasionally mentioned in academic literature on early twentieth-century Russian and Soviet literary and linguistic scholarship, he has remained virtually unknown outside a small circle of specialists. Eclipsed by such luminaries as Viktor Shklovsky, Yury Tynyanov, Boris Eikhenbuam, Roman Jakobson, and others who came to represent the so-called 'Russian formalist' movement, which he co-founded and which revolutionized the way we look at and interpret literature and culture to this day, Yakubinsky has been relegated to the footnotes of modern intellectual history. Thus, the book you are now holding in your hands can be viewed as a recovery mission of sorts, aiming to give a powerful, unduly forgotten thinker the historical credit he deserves by making his work widely available in English, and to broaden and enrich our overall perspective on and understanding of the vagaries of modern literary and cultural theory. Together with Yakubinsky's book-length essay *On Dialogic Speech*—originally published in the Soviet Union in 1923 and first published in English in 2016—the present volume gathers some of Yakubinsky's historically and critically most relevant writings, giving the non-Russian-speaking reader the opportunity to engage with this influential mind first-hand.

*

Born in Kiev in 1892, Lev Petrovich Yakubinsky studied philology and linguistics at Kiev and Petersburg Universities from 1909 to 1915, during a period of change and renewal in Russian linguistics, which had up to then been dominated by neogrammarian positivism and historicism. Originating in Leipzig, Germany, in the 1870s, and subsequently making its way to Russia, the neogrammarian school—represented, among others, by Eduard Sievers (1850-1932) and August Leskien (1840-1916) in Germany, and Fillip Fortunatov (1848-1914) in Russia—postulated the existence of *a priori* phonological laws and held that the description of the historical transformations of language(s) should take precedence over the investigation of living speech in its concrete, dynamic and generative, aspects. This abstract, 'de-humanized' approach to our most important and ubiquitous social and cognitive medium was eagerly contested by a group of young scholars and critics—no doubt inspired and fueled by the fermenting cultural-political atmosphere leading up to and surrounding the October Revolution of 1917—who were far more interested in the functional and social diversity of language as an individual and collective activity.

"The word is now dead," proclaimed Viktor Shklovsky, one of the group's most vociferous members, as early as 1914 in his famous manifesto "The Resurrection of the Word": "We have lost our connection to the world, we no longer feel it ... Only the creation of new forms ... will restore our lived experience of the world [oshshyushsheniye mira], resurrect things, and kill pessimism." (Shklovsky, by the way, was not alone in issuing a clarion call in the name of restoring "our lived experience of the world" by means of language. At roughly the same time, another young literary formation, the so-called Acmeists—in explicit opposition to the Symbolist doctrine of *a realibus ad realiora [from the real to the ideal]*—campaigned for exactly the same goal: "our lived experience of the world [oshshyushsheniye mira]," as Mandelstam famously put it in his 1913 poetic manifesto "The Morning of Acmeism.")

What better way to make good on Shklovsky's ethical imperative, insofar as it is premised on breathing new life into language, than to begin by investigating the most self-conscious and self-reflexive form of linguistic activity: poetry (and literature more generally). The founding by Shklovsky and a cluster of friends and colleagues at Petersburg University of the Society for the Study of Poetic Language [OPO-YAZ: Obshchestvo po Izucheniyu Poeticheskogo Yazyka] in 1916—which, in dialogue with the so-called Moscow Linguistic Circle, developed what came to be known as 'Russian formalism'—was designed to do just that: teach us to see and feel the world anew—"as if for the first time," as Shklovsky wrote in his seminal essay "Art as Device" (1917)—by teaching us to attend to language in a new way. And this new way of looking at language, in turn, which would be different from previous linguistic approaches, hinged on the categorical distinction between *poetic* and *practical* language. More specifically: on the distinction between the two modes of language not in respect to their *what* so much as in respect to their *how*; not in respect to *content* and its variously conceived referential relation to the world (a question sufficiently dealt with by Aristotle and his followers) so much as in respect to *form*—in respect, that is, to the *technical ways*, the material, semiotic *devices* (phonological, morphological, syntactic, grammatical, rhetorical, etc.) that arguably distinguish literary from ordinary or practical language (and, in turn, obviously impact content). "The methodological distinction and juxtaposition of poetic and practical language," Boris Eikhenbaum summed up in his retrospective 1925 essay "The Theory of the *Formal Method*," "served as the foundational principle underlying the formalist approach as a whole."

Enter Yakubinsky: for, as Eikhenbaum observes in the same essay, it was none other than "Yakubinsky who introduced this distinction," thus laying the methodological cornerstone for Russian formalism. Shklovsky, too, underscores Yakubinsky's role as the movement's methodological progenitor: referencing his work multiple times in "Art as Device," Shklovsky credits Yakubinsky with the insight that "the two languages [poetic and practical] do not coincide" and that "the laws governing poetic language are diametrically opposed to those governing practical language." The text in which Yakubinsky first posited and elaborated this signal dichotomy appeared in OPOYAZ's inaugural anthology *Essays on the Theory of Poetic Language* in 1916 and was titled "On the Sounds of Poetic Language."

*

Given that Russian formalism constitutes a central historical-conceptual matrix and reference point for such later, historically imbricated, schools of thought as, among others, structuralism (its immediate successor), post-structuralism, deconstruction, and new historicism—all of which in one way or another appropriated, further developed, modified, critiqued, or departed from it—Yakubinsky must be considered a true "initiator of discursive practices," to use Michel Foucault's phrase. As Foucault explains in "What Is an Author" (1969): what distinguishes "initiators of discursive practices" from other types of authorship—novelists, say—is that they not only "make a certain number of analogies possible" by providing patterns that can be variously adopted by others; but, more importantly, that "they also make a certain number of differences possible" by "opening up a space for discourses different from theirs, yet belonging to the field which they have initiated." Precisely this kind of space was opened up, if not exclusively of course, by Yakubinsky's "On the Sounds of Poetic Language"—a founding document of modern poetics and literary theory—which is made available in English for the first time.

*

What was it about Yakubinsky's categorical distinction between poetic and practical language that made "On the Sounds of Poetic Language" such a key text? After all, the conception of literature as different or deviating from ordinary language in itself would certainly not have been news given its long tradition from Aristotle through the modern period.

What made Yakubinsky's particular take on this subject arguably so transformative, was the prism through which he chose to refract it—linguistics coupled with psychology and epistemology:

> In practical verbal thinking, we don't focus on the sounds of words; we don't consciously pay attention to them, they don't possess independent value, merely serving communication. It is precisely this lack of conscious attention to

sounds in practical language that explains why many slips of the tongue go unnoticed, and why we can easily get away with sloppy articulation, slurring endings or entire syllables ... When it comes to poetic language, the situation is reversed: we do become consciously aware of the material texture of words, we are enjoined to focus on their sounds above all ... A poetic utterance's rhythmicality, for instance, bespeaks the conscious experiencing of sound in the process of poetic creation (poetic verbal thinking) ... rhythm in verse depends on the syllables' specific phonic make-up, for example on their consonant count. Consequently, our perception of and attention to rhythm in poetry is inseparable from our conscious awareness of its sound patterns.

Yakubinsky's explanation as to why poetic and practical language—which he characterizes as types of verbal thinking—need to be considered distinct modes communication sets the stage for at least two of formalism's and structuralism's defining claims about language and art: it prefigures Shklovsky's immensely influential notion of "demamiliarization" as the most basic aesthetic "device"; and it also anticipates Roman Jakobson's key structuralist concept of the "poetic function" as the dominant linguistic function in literature.

Taking his cue from Yakubinsky's discussion of the psychological-cognitive dimension of our engagement with literature—which emphasizes conscious experiencing and awareness, as well as our focus on the words' very materiality—Shklovsky writes in "Art as Device" (in arguably one of the most well-known paragraphs in modern aesthetic theory):

> In order to restore our lived experience of the world and feel things again, in order to make a stone a stone again, we have something called art. The goal of art is to transform our experience of things from [simply] recognizing them to [consciously] seeing them; the device of art consists in the 'defamiliarization' of things and in the complication of forms, which slows down perception and makes it more difficult ... [I should note that Shklovsky also mentions another, highly technical, essay by Yakubinsky as a conceptual reference point: "The Accumulation

of Identical Liquids in Practical and Poetic Language," published in 1917. Because this piece presupposes the reader's ability to follow intricate linguistic description in several languages, including German and Russian, however, it is not included in the present volume.]

If it is the process of slowing down perception—which means taking the time to *consciously* and *attentively* look at what is before us—that makes the familiar, the "unnoticed," unfamiliar and noteworthy, then Yakubinsky can plausibly be said to have implicitly adumbrated the principle of "defamiliarization."

Concomitantly, if what distinguishes poetic from practical language above all is the former's ability to draw our attention to itself in its very materiality, then Yakubinsky can be said to have anticipated Jakobson's famous definition in "Linguistics and Poetics" (1960) of the "poetic function" as "the set (*Einstellung* [Germ.: attitude]) toward the message as such, focus on the message for its own sake."

*

After the Russian Revolution, Yakubinsky gradually moved away from his fellow formalists' preoccupation with poetry and literature. Aligning himself with the new Communist regime, which frowned upon the formalists' lack of interest in the ideological and political aspects of literature and art, Yakubinsky turned to exploring the social dimension of language in its "phenomenal immediacy," as he puts it in his groundbreaking 1923 essay "On Dialogic Speech."

The very first study devoted entirely to the forms of speech in their concrete intersubjective manifestations, "On Dialogic Speech" is also the first study addressing the linguistic, psychophysiological, pragmatic, semantic and sociopolitical aspects of dialogue, which Yakubinsky implicitly credits with the weakening of authority and power (as opposed to the natural "alliance that monologue has with authority"). As I have suggested in my foreword to the first English edition of "On Dialogic Speech" (2016), Yakubinsky's essay can thus be said to anticipate the Bakhtin circle's seminal writings on the transformative power of dialogue, as well as such disciplines as socio-linguistics, pragmatics, and cultural and postcolonial studies, insofar as the latter appropriate and strategically implement the concept and potential of dialogue as a liberating force. (Ironically, in coming down on the side of dialogue as opposed to monologue, "On Dialogic Speech" ostensibly undermines its author's own ideological position.)

"On Dialogic Speech" can also be said to describe and theorize, *avant la lettre*, our contemporary culture of texting, tweeting, messaging and emailing—the twenty-first-century equivalents of "passing notes" (in class, meetings, and so on), which Yakubinsky singles out as a unique hybrid "between mediated (written) and unmediated (properly dialogic) communication."

*

For the remainder of his life, until his death in 1945, Yakubinsky worked mainly on problems in linguistics sanctioned by the powers that be. Expertly navigating the political waters of Leninism and Stalinism, Yakubinsky became a successful, highly respected professor of linguistics at a number of Soviet institutions—including the Volodarsky Institute for Agitation—and penned essays such as "Lenin on the 'Revolutionary Phrase'" (1926), "The Language of the Proletariat" (1931), "The Russian Language in the Age of Proletarian Dictatorship" (1931), "On the Language of the Classes" (1932), and "Soviet Linguistics" (1934), to name only a few.

Among these later works, all of which toe the Communist Party line, one stands out, however: "Ferdinand de Saussure on the Impossibility of Language Politics" (1931). And even though this essay, too, is written from an ideologically invested position, and could thus be accused of tendentiousness, the critique it brings to bear on Ferdinand de Saussure's (1857-1913) posthumously published *Course in General Linguistics* (1916)—one of the most influential theoretical works of the modern era—is not in any way vitiated by Yakubinsky's political views. For in his close reading of Saussure these views are relevant only insofar as they are premised on the fundamental notion that political change can be effected through language; and since this notion is certainly not unique to Communism—far from it: one could argue that all political change begins with and in language, and depends on it—the critique Yakubinsky levels against Saussure reveals itself as issuing, above all, from a logically and factually plausible vantage point that could be—and indeed has been—occupied by other critics wishing to address Saussure's vexing inconsistencies.

What Yakubinsky takes exception to in particular is Saussure's postulate that language "eludes our will" and is thus beyond our control, which, in turn, entails the "impossibility of a revolution in language." For "if Saussure is right," Yakubinsky notes, "then any organized intervention in the linguistic [and, by extension, political] process, any organized societal attempt at impacting the direction of this process, that is, any language politics become impossible." And that's something, it is safe to say, that not only Yakubinsky disagrees with: over half a century after Yakubinsky's critique of Saussure's perceived 'quietism', Derek Attridge—in one of the most insightful and subtle readings of Saussure, titled "Language as History/History as Language: Saussure and the Romance of Etymology" (1987)—would speak precisely to this issue. After citing the same passage from the *Course* as Yakubinsky—"Not only would an individual, even if he wanted to, be utterly incapable of changing the choice that has been made by language, but the social mass, too, has no power over a single word"—Attridge comments: "There is, in fact, plenty of evidence that languages do change as a result of ... intervention: one example is the existence of spellings and often pronunciations which reflect 're-forms' ..."

Yakubinsky doesn't stop here, though. Intent on understanding how Saussure could have possibly arrived at such a "misguided" view, he proceeds—in a radical about-face in his own thinking—to a full-scale deconstruction of the basic tenets of Saussure's linguistic enterprise as a whole (and thus, by implication, of some of the conceptual underpinnings of much subsequent theory), attacking each of Saussure's four "most essential" arguments, "on which all others depend," concerning our "powerlessness" vis-à-vis language, namely:

(1) the "arbitrary character of the sign" (which, by the way—as Saussure, a great connoisseur of the Romantic tradition, certainly knew—Wilhelm von Humboldt had already adumbrated in *On the Structural Differences of Human Languages and Their Influence on the Intellectual Evolution of Humankind* [1836], when analyzing the ostensibly arbitrary "articulation" of "thought" and "sound");

(2) the "multitude of signs necessary for the constitution any language";

(3) the "overly complex character of the system";

(4) the "resistance of collective inertia to all linguistic innovation."

Having subscribed, in "On the Sounds of Poetic Language," to "the common view of contemporary linguistics," namely, that "we have no reason at all to assume that there is an internal connection between the sound of a word and its meaning" and that this "connection is determined through association by contiguity, and [is] merely factual, rather than natural"—in other words, that it is "arbitrary"—Yakubinsky now argues the opposite: the "true nature of the connection" between a word and its meaning is "completely different from Saussure's description of it"; "the formula of the 'arbitrariness of the sign' ... as well as Saussure's theory ... as a whole are misguided," for the "connection between a word and its meaning is historically conditioned" and, thus, *not* at all "arbitrary."

Saussure's second error, according to Yakubinsky, consists in positing a functional (and factual) link between the (potentially) infinite quantity of signs in a language and its amenability to displacement by its speakers. Why should a "multitude of signs" in itself prevent the latter? It might require effort, certainly, but effort does not necessarily translate into impossibility. Why, Yakubinsky asks, should "a partial transformation of language by its speakers" be impossible, for instance?

Saussure commits a related error in suggesting that the complexity of language as a system represents an impenetrable bulwark against user intervention. Why, though, should systemic complexity and innovation be mutually exclusive? Mainly, Saussure argues—and Yakubinsky doesn't fail to swiftly eviscerate this dubious claim—due to the majority of speakers' "ignorance"and presumed lack of interest (and wherewithal) to engage in sustained "reflection" on the workings of language, which Saussure adduces as a precondition for its transformation. (Here, too, by the way, the degree of potential difficulty and effort involved does not at all entail the impossibility of the project, or doom it to failure.)

Finally, claiming that a community's collective resistant inertia presents an insurmountable obstacle to linguistic initiative is historically (and logically) untenable—resistance, after all, is known to have been broken on occasion, as Yakubinsky amply documents with particular attention to the language reforms that created contemporary Czech.

*

What makes Yakubinsky's take on Saussure so significant today, however, I believe, is not his critique *per se* so much as its 'prescience'—its 'foreshadowing' of similar or related criticisms brought to bear on the Swiss linguist decades later. "… let us ask," Derek Attridge enjoins, implicitly articulating the concerns of an entire generation of post-Saussurean critics, "how we might acknowledge the feedback of history into the here and now, and the determination of language not by 'blind' forces [as Saussure suggests] but by human, social, and political agency, both conscious and unconscious. To do so would mean regarding language as inherently unstable, internally (and eternally) shifting …" Yakubinsky, it would appear, had already accomplished this task of "regarding language as inherently unstable" half a century earlier.

*

One can't help but wonder whether the trajectory of modern poetics and cultural theory might have been different (if ever so slightly)—and if so, how?—had Yakubinsky's writings been part of the global critical conversation all along? We will never know, of course. But at least, now that they are finally available in English, we can revisit some of the stops along the way and reexamine them in the new light provided by Yakubinsky's pioneering work.

*

A final remark on the third text featured in this book, "Where Do Poems Come from?": this short companion piece to "On the Sounds of Poetic Language" shows a side of Yakubinsky that doesn't come out in his other writings—playful, humorous, tongue-in-cheek. Its heavy reliance on Freud is especially noteworthy given its historical-political context in the early years of the Soviet Union: soon enough psychoanalysis would be routed as bourgeois anathema.

A Note on Translation

With very few exceptions pertaining to "On the Sounds of Poetic Language," the essays here gathered represent complete English versions of Yakubinsky's Russian originals.

For the contemporary English reader's convenience, I have omitted a very small number of passages from "On the sounds of Poetic Language" that reiterate, repeat, or provide additional illustrations for points already made with sufficient clarity; that only work in Russian for prosodic, phonological, or morphological reasons, and whose absence does not in any way detract from Yakubinsky's argument, substantively or otherwise.

All translations from French are my own.

On the Sounds of Poetic Language

"O zvukakh stikhotvornogo yazyka." *Soborniki po teorii poeticheskogo yazyka [Essays on the Theory of Poetic Language], vol. 1* (St. Petersburg, 1916), pp. 6-30.

The manifestations of language must be classified according to our goals in employing the verbal means at our disposal in a given situation. If we employ these means solely for the practical purpose of communication, then we are dealing with the system of *practical language* (practical verbal thinking), where the linguistic means (sounds, morphological elements, etc.) don't possess independent value. But there are other language systems where practical considerations take a back seat, without completely disappearing, and words and meanings themselves acquire independent value.

Contemporary linguistics focuses almost exclusively on practical language. The study of other language systems, however, is equally relevant. In this essay, I elaborate some of the psycho-phonetic features of the language system at work in the process of poetic creation. I conditionally call this system *poetic language* (poetic verbal thinking).

*

In practical verbal thinking, we don't focus on the sounds of words; we don't consciously pay attention to them, they don't possess independent value, merely serving communication. It is precisely this lack of conscious attention to sounds in practical language that explains why many slips of the tongue go unnoticed, and why we can easily get away with sloppy articulation, slurring endings or entire syllables—something students of acting in particular have to grapple with.

There is yet another, more complex aspect to the phonetics of practical language, which Jan Baudouin de Courtenay calls the non-coincidence of our articulatory intent and its actual execution: it consists in our failure to articulate what we actually set out to articulate—as when, due to physiological conditions affecting our speech organs, we say 'life' instead of 'live' (as in 'live theater') without really noticing the difference between the voiced *v* and the voiceless *f*, which is possible only because we don't pay close attention to sounds in ordinary speech. In practical language, then, a word's semantic aspect—its meaning—takes precedence over its phonic aspect—its sound—which is perfectly understandable, since we pay attention to differences in pronunciation in ordinary speech mostly when these differences imply differences in meaning.

When it comes to poetic language, the situation is reversed: we do become consciously aware of the material texture of words, we are enjoined to focus on their sounds above all. On this subject, testimonies provided by poets themselves based on self-observation go a long way. A poetic utterance's rhythmicality, for instance, bespeaks the conscious experiencing of sound in the process of poetic creation (poetic verbal thinking). As has often been remarked, rhythm in verse depends on the syllables' specific phonic make-up, for example on their consonant count. Consequently, our perception of and attention to rhythm in poetry is inseparable from our conscious awareness of its sound patterns.

Phonic correspondences in verse (alliterations, assonances, rhymes, etc.) may or may not be intended by the poet; in the former case, we again witness a conscious focus on sounds in speech: rhyme, for one, would hardly make sense if our relation to sounds in poetic and practical verbal thinking, respectively, were the same.

*

In one of his letters, Aleksey Konstantinovich Tolstoy speaks precisely to this issue when he addresses Ivan Turgenev's criticism of the presumably "limping rhymes" in his (Tolstoy's) 1859 poem "John of Damascus":

> We still have to address Turgenev's accusation of my limping rhymes! Could it be that Turgenev belongs to the French school, which aims to satisfy the eye rather than the ear? ... The vowels at the end of rhymes don't really matter if unstressed, I believe. The consonants count and

supply the rhymes … It seems to me that only an inexperienced ear will demand matching vowels in rhymes; and it will do so only because it makes concessions to the eye. I may be wrong, but it's something I feel deeply—a consequence of my euphonic constitution, and you know how demanding my ear is.

Tolstoy's observations are highly significant: they document the poet's hyperconscious attention to sound in the process of poetic creation. It's perfectly plausible to assume that other poets have the same conscious relation to sound in verse, often aiming to establish phonic equivalences that don't play much of a role in ordinary speech (practical verbal thinking).

*

Let me repeat my conclusion: sounds in practical language (practical verbal thinking) don't possess independent value, they don't draw our attention, and we are not consciously aware of them. In poetic language (poetic verbal thinking), conversely, sounds do become the focus of our attention; they acquire independent value, and we become consciously aware of them.

*

Closely linked to our heightened attention to sounds is our emotional relation to them. A good number of poets have documented their emotional relation to sounds.

Prince Vyazemsky, for instance, writes in his *Autobiography*:

> Reading the *Moscow News*, I would often lose myself in wine merchants' price lists, being drawn especially to some of the wines' poetic designations, such as *Lacryma-Christi* and similarly euphonic names. Perhaps these names awakened and resonated with my inner poetic self … I also remember that even earlier in life, as a child, I drew immense pleasure from spelling out letters and combining them into distinct sounds, which caressed my musical ear … It wasn't the poems' meanings so much as their melodious, undulating rhythms that mesmerized me.

Mikhail Lermontov, too, provides compelling evidence on this topic. He frequently writes of the sounds of words, separating them from their meanings. Thus, a variant of his poem "Angel" reads:

The soul settled down amid earthly creation
But it felt estranged in this world.
Of one thing only it dreamed: sacred sounds,
Their meaning it did not remember.

Or take the following early draft of Lermontov's famous 1840 poem "There are words—their meaning dark or insignificant":

There are sounds, their meaning unimportant,
Shunned by the masses in their pride,
Forgetting them is not an option,
One with the soul they are—like life …

Nikolay Gogol puts it particularly well in his 1846 essay "On the Ultimate Essence and Singularity of Russian Poetry":

Euphony is not as unimportant a matter as those unfamiliar with poetry believe. By the strains of euphony, as if by the beautiful melodies of a mother's lullabies, common folk are rocked to sleep—like infants, even before they have learned the different meanings of the lullabies' words … Euphony is as necessary as burning incense in church, which primes the soul to hearken to something higher even before mass has begun.

And here's also Innokenty Annensky's poetic reflection on the sounds in the word 'nevoz-mozhno [impossible]' from his posthumous 1910 collection *The Cypress Box*:

There are words—their scent, like a flower's,
Is tender and stirringly white,
But there's none among them that's as sad
And as tender as you: *nevozmozhno*.

Ere I knew it, I already loved
Your velvet-enveloppèd sounds:
The graves' distant flicker I saw
And the whiteness of hands in the dusk.

In the white Chrysanthemums' wreath, though,
Before oblivion's first onset, I learned
To discern the fragrances wafting
From your *ve*, and your *ze*, and your *em*.

*

Focusing on the sounds of speech goes hand in hand with a specific emotional relation to them: "The most familiar, common phenomena and sounds," Ivan Konevskoy observes, "reveal secret passages and unsuspected depths once we allow ourselves to delve deeper into them, and for a little longer, rather than merely skating along their surfaces" (*Poems and Prose* [1904]).

*

We can often observe an emotional relation to the sounds of unfamiliar words—from another language, for example, or nonsense words—where our attention is willy-nilly directed toward their phonic texture.

Let me quote a passage from William James' *Principles of Psychology* (1890), which deals with the question of our apprehension of the sounds of a foreign language:

Our own language would sound very different to us if we heard it without understanding, as we hear a foreign tongue. Rises and falls of voice, odd sibilants and other consonants, would fall on our ear in a way of which we can now form no notion. Frenchmen say that English sounds to them like the *gazouillement des oiseaux*—an impression which it certainly makes on no native ear. Many of us English would describe the sound of Russian in similar terms. All of us are conscious of the strong inflections of voice and explosives and gutturals of German speech in a way in which no German can be conscious of them.

But even when we have mastered a foreign language to a greater or lesser degree, its sounds continue to exert an emotional influence.

In his *Treatise on French Stylistics* (1909), French linguist Charles Bally also comments on this phenomenon, noting that the impact of a word's sound is independent of its meaning even if we know the latter:

> Of course, when we hear a foreign language, where our associations between the meaning of a word and the word itself have not yet solidified, our mind involuntarily enhances the musical effects where they actually exist, and perceives them even where they don't exist. Associations that we can barely capture emerge, in which individual impressions reminiscent of 'folk etymology' play a significant role. The sound of the verb *zwitschern*, for instance, is certainly more striking to me than to a German——an illu-

sion that is at least a little bit rooted in the word's meaning. But what about a word like *erklecklich* [Germ.: considerable], which to me sounds peculiar, almost ridiculous—an impression not borne out by the word's meaning at all!

That we experience sounds emotionally is also aptly captured in Edgar Allan Poe's "To Marie Louise" (1848):

Two words—two foreign, soft dissyllables —
Two gentle sounds made only to be murmured
By angels dreaming in the moon-lit "dew
That hands like chains of pearl on Hermon hill"
Have stirred from out of the abysses of his heart
Unthought-like thoughts—scarcely the shades
                                        [of thought—

*

The phenomenon of exposing the phonetic aspects of words is also often accompanied by an emotional experience of their sounds, which draw our attention. Here's how William James describes this phenomenon:

This is probably the reason why, if we look at an isolated printed word and repeat it long enough, it ends by assuming an entirely unnatural aspect. Let the reader try this with any word on this page. He will soon begin to wonder if it can possibly be the word he has been using all his life with that meaning. It stares at him from the paper like a glass eye, with no speculation in it. Its body is indeed there, but its soul has fled. It is reduced, by this new way of attending to it, to its essential nudity. We never before attended to it in this way, but habitually got it clad with its meaning the moment we caught sight of it, and rapidly passed from it to the other words in the phrase. We apprehended it, in short, with a cloud of associates, and thus perceiving it, we felt it quite otherwise than as we feel it now divested and alone.

This phenomenon of 'exposing' a word is fairly widespread, and probably all of us have had the opportunity to witness it at one time or another.

Let me provide two examples of this type of exposure (both from Mikhail Kuzmin's 1910 novel *Gentle Joseph*):

'Rome'? How beautiful: rounded, dome-like … Joseph walked over to the window, and looking at the vanishing line of roofs and buildings, at the crosses of churches far-away and close-by, at the wide-open sky, he began repeating: 'Rome, Rome, Rome …' until the sounds had lost their meaning and his soul was filled with a vastness resembling the sky or the dome of a cathedral.

How wondrous: you will understand everything in a word once you start repeating it, once it enters your soul. Look at the flower … and repeat its name a hundred times, and continue looking at it with all your being, and you will understand what the flower means, and you will see how it lives, as if you had read all the books that have been written about it, but you won't be able tell us about it …

*

The ancients, too, knew about our emotional relation to sounds: the letter Sigma, for example, was considered unpleasant and far from beautiful, producing a feeling of annoyance if used repeatedly, which is why it was employed rarely and with caution by some, and why there are classical fables that are entirely devoid of this letter.

Poetic language, then, reveals our emotional relation to its sounds by dint of its ability to draw our attention to its phonic texture—a crucial fact if we wish to grasp the connection between sound and sense in poetry.

*

In practical language, we have no reason at all to assume that there is an internal connection between the sound of a word and its meaning. This connection is determined through association by contiguity, and it is merely factual, rather than natural, as Antoine Meillet has rightly pointed out. For if there were a necessary, internal connection between a word's sound and its meaning, phonic shifts and variations in words that don't in any way affect or alter their meaning would be incomprehensible. In his *Introduction to the Comparative Study of Indo-European Languages* (1903), Meillet gives the following example: "*Horse* (English); *loshad'* (Russian); *cheval* (French); *Pferd* (German); *asp* (Persian);

ji (Armenian)—whoever doesn't already understand that these different terms mean the same animal will certainly not be convinced otherwise." Meillet's insight, which expresses the common view of contemporary linguistics, necessarily applies to practical language. But what about poetic language?

*

As noted earlier, poetic language is characterized by our emotional relation to its sound texture. According to Wilhelm Wundt's *Foundations of Psychology* (1896), the emotions thus triggered by individual sounds and sound sequences may vary in quality and kind on the "pleasure / displeasure," "calm / agitation" "relaxation / tension" spectra. Whereby emotions triggered by the sounds of poetry ought not to run counter to the emotions triggered by its content, and *vice versa*. And if that's the case, then this means that poetry's content and sound texture are emotionally interdependent. Consequently, poets select sounds and sound sequences based on their perceived emotional suitedness to the imagery at hand, and *vice versa*.

It seems to me that these fairly elementary observations on the interdependence of sound and sense in poetry provide a certain theoretical foundation for many a poet's testimony (especially in our time) on the unity of form and content in poetry.

*

The link between a poem's content and its sound texture is not exclusively based on our emotional relation to sounds but also on the fact that our speech organs are capable of expressive movement.

As far as the expressive involvement or our speech physiology is concerned, we need to consider the breathing organs and larynx (vocal cords, etc.) on the one hand, and elements such as the soft palate, mandible, lips, and tongue on the other.

The emotionally expressive role of the breathing organs and larynx is obvious: a whole range of intonational details—pitch, tonal intensity, expressivity, etc.—is entirely determined by them. The expressive role of the other parts might not be as obvious; however, there is no doubt that they, too, often accompany and contribute to the expression of emotion. "That our articulatory muscles do not in any way fall behind the other muscles is self-evident," Tadeusz Zelinsky pertinently observes in *Wilhelm Wundt and the Psychology of Language* (1911). "Think of Gogol's Akaky Akakyevich [the protagonist of the novella *The Overcoat*] and how he 'chuckled, blinked, and moved his lips' while writing. We all know that our lips can, and often do, express what and how we feel in a given moment: smiling, distorted, pouting, pursed, etc."

*

The role of the soft palate is mostly negative: certain emotional states are characterized by the fact that the soft palate is not engaged at all and that as a result our speech acquires a 'nasal' quality ('speaking through the nose').

Turgenev is a rich source of material on the subject of nasal pronunciation as a function of emotion. Commenting on the "disdainful tone of voice" of one of his characters in *A Sportman's Sketches* (1852), Turgenev writes: "The stranger was talking incredibly fast, incoherently, and through his nose." (Speaking through ones nose as a mark of disdain and condescension is sufficiently common.) And in the 1874 novella *Punin and Baburin*, the voice of the "grandmother" becomes more nasal as her displeasure and irritation grow: "Enough, enough already—interrupted the grandmother, and—having thought for a while—said in a nasal voice that it was always a bad sign ... " Similarly, in Turgenev's 1860 novel *On the Eve* we read:

> 'You don't know what Milonov the poet has written about me?' the old man asked, working himself into a state of agitation. 'No wedding candles have been lit'—he began in a sing-song voice, breathing all the vowels through his nose and pronouncing the syllables 'ding' and 'can' *à la française* as 'daing' and 'cong' ...

The mandible's expressive significance is most salient when we clench our teeth. We can hear it because everything we enunciate appears constrained, muted, stifled; open vowels sound choked. Expressions such as 'speak through one's teeth' or 'mutter between one's teeth' neatly capture this phenomenon. This type of muffled speech is due to the expressive movement—or rather its absence—of the mandible; it is often used to great acoustic effect.

The expressive role of the tongue, finally, is yet again pointedly captured by Turgenev: in the novella *First Love* (1860), the protagonist Vladimir "anxiously mutters his words," which is the direct result of the tongue's obstruction of normal articulation. Similarly, *On the Eve*'s Bersenev "would speak more slowly and fall into a kind of mutter whenever he spoke to a woman ..."

*

In practical speech, where our attention is not focused on the sounds themselves and where we aren't typically conscious of emotionally conditioned sound shifts, we easily tolerate modifications in the phonic texture of speech (which are caused by the expressive movements of our speech organs). It's different in poetic speech: for here we emphatically focus on sounds; here phonic shifts and modifications would not only *not* go unnoticed, but some of them might actually sound unnatural, if not impossible (and perhaps even ridiculous). That's why poets endeavor to choose words whose pronunciation will physiologically correspond with their overall expressive goals. When we feel something that makes us smile (distend our lips sideways), we will obviously avoid sounds requiring pointing our lips, such as *o* or *u*.

*

A poet's attunement to the activity of his speech organs can trigger corresponding aural (phonic) 'ideas', in which case a poem's sound structure is tied to the poet's phonic imagination, and the sequence of speech organ movements or the sequence of phonic imaginings marks the inception of poetic thinking. That's what poets mean when they say that poetry begins with sound. Schiller, for instance, would often hear "a poem's music in [his] soul first, before having a clear idea of its content" (cited in Ernest Dupré and Marcel Nathan, *Le langage musical: Étude medico-psychologique* [1911]).

Let's hear Gogol once more, this time from his 1834 essay "On Ukranian Songs":

In these songs, the most colorful and true images are coupled with the most resonant music. These songs are not composed with quill in hand, not on paper, not mathematically, but in a trance, in a state of oblivion, when the soul itself sings and all the members of the body attain a freedom that breaks the shackles of passivity and habit as the arms fly upward and the singer is carried far away on the waves of ecstasy. This can be observed even in the most plangent songs whose despairing sounds painfully touch the heart. They could never emanate from the soul of a person in a normal state, soberly considering the content at hand. Only when the wine has jumbled and destroyed the prosaic order of thought, when our thoughts' internal dissonance resonates with its inexplicable and strange inner consonance, then—in this majestic, rather than merely joyful, state of intoxication—the soul, enigmatically, overflows with barely bearable lamentations. Gone are reason and awareness! The singer's entire mysterious being is thirsting for sound, sound alone. That's why these songs' poetry cannot be captured, why it mesmerizes, why it is full of grace—like music. The poetry

of thought, on the other hand, is far more accessible to everyone than the poetry of sound, or,
to put it more aptly, the poetry of poetry. Only
the chosen, the true poet himself understands it
in his soul; and that's why the best songs often
remain in obscurity, whereas the more common
ones win our approval through their content.

*

Even if there happens to occur no movement of
the speech organs in the process of poetic creation (poetic verbal thinking), however, the
poem's sound structure will be aligned with and
reflect its emotional matrix. For even if no expressive physical movement accompanies a giv-
en emotion——as we transition to movement
more generally (while the emotion is still lasting), we can only move in ways that don't run
counter to, and indeed approximate, those
movements that would have expressed the given
emotion in the first place. Thus, while no physical movement may have occurred in the process
of experiencing a given emotion——as soon as we
feel the need to move (all the while continuing
to experience the emotion), we might, for in-

stance, move forward rather than back, or forcefully rather than listlessly. And forward and backward movements certainly mean different things as expressions of emotion. When it comes to our speech organs, this means for example that we move our tongue forward when articulating sounds such as *e* and *i*, while moving it back when articulating vowels such as *o* and *ou*. Which yet again underscores the difference among vowel groups in emotional range and effect—something poets and theoreticians alike have frequently remarked on.

*

In conclusion, I would like to repeat my main insights concerning the sounds of poetic language: in poetic verbal thinking, we become consciously aware of sounds, which goes hand in hand with our emotional relation to them; this in turn entails the interdependence of content and form in poetry—its sound texture, more specifically—which is supported by the expressive movement of our speech organs.

Where Do Poems Come from?

"Otkuda berutsya stikhi." *Knizhny ugol* 7 (1921): 21-25.

In this short essay, I will not be concerned with the question, "How and when did poetry originate in history?" I will, therefore, leave our apelike ancestors alone, as well as the German Karl Bücher's *Labor and Rhythm* (1896) and similar grand forays, and restrict myself to the simple question: how does it happen that in certain, rare moments in his humdrum existence, citizen X, who is perfectly capable of expressing himself in the most ordinary Russian, French, German, etc., discovers within himself the poetic "source of limpid, simple sounds" (Lermontov). Where do citizen X's poems come from?

*

The question having been posed with sufficient clarity, let's now try and answer it.

Let's also agree from start that whatever it is that distinguishes poetry as a verbal art in its own right resides in the phonic aspect of speech. That much is clear. For even if poetry contains something beyond sound, that something emerges, exists, and is perceived solely owing and in relation to its sounds. Sound determines poetry. If we take sound out of poetry, there will be no poetry left.

And so: phonic monism in the study of verse is what we stand for. Let's move along.

*

What are the phonic characteristics of poetry?

1. Rhythm, meter, measure.

2. Phonic relations (associations) between words and combinations of words: repetitions, alliterations, assonances, etc.

3. The phonic structure's axiological independence both in respect to articulation and sound—hence all that babble about euphony (often misguided, but facts are facts).

4. The emotional significance of sounds and sound combinations: sounds and sound combinations express emotion; the content of the

phonetics of poetry depends on its emotional tonality; plenty of verbiage has been generated on this subject (including by yours truly); still, you should take a look at my essay "On the Sounds of Poetic Language."

5. The complexity and "heightened difficulty" (Shklovsky) of the sound texture of poetry in comparison with ordinary speech.

*

Poetry is not the only form of speech where sounds reign supreme.

First, there are dreams (not always, of course): I dream of Lila, then lilies, then lullabies—all this is sufficiently well known; words connect through sounds, thus determining the dream content. Second, there is mental illness: some mentally ill deliver long, incoherent tirades (as can be expected) that are nonetheless deeply coherent and well measured in terms of their phonic structure. Third, there is ecstasy and trance: think, for instance, of the practice of glossolalia in certain cults.

All of these phenomena have been explained by Sigmund Freud; he juxtaposes them with the "babble" of early childhood, which is gradually supplanted by "conscious" speech.

*

There is no experience or impression that doesn't leave a trace, a memory in the human psyche, faint and barely discernable though it may be; this also applies to the verbal impressions of childhood. Not useful in everyday life, these impressions tend to lie dormant on the bottom of Lethe; but in certain irregular, abnormal mental states they can rise to the surface. As Freud has noted, this is true not only of verbal impressions but of any early childhood impression whatsoever (sexual, etc.). Dreams, ecstasy, and mental illness are such irregular, abnormal mental states. In these states, immemorial verbal impressions from early childhood rise to the surface and in combination with conscious adult speech (or whatever is left of it in these states) produce new forms of verbal expression.

It is very interesting to apply this method of explication to poetry: all the more so given that poetic speech has much more in common with infantile speech than with the language of ecstasy or mental illness.

*

What, then, are the characteristics of infantile speech?

1. The rhythmicality of its monologic babble.

2. The prevalence of phonic assonances: repetition, doubling, etc.

3. The fact that to the child this babble is valuable in itself: the child babbles for the sake of babbling and derives great pleasure from this babble, both from the very act of babbling and from hearing and listening to it.

4. The emotional significance of the child's phonic expressivity: initially, the child only 'speaks', emits sounds, as a way of expressing and articulating emotion.

5. The phonic complexity of the child's babble and first verbal articulations more generally: the child articulates sounds and sound combinations that it will take a long time to 'relearn' as it transitions to conscious speech; some of these sounds, moreover, will no longer be used at all in ordinary, cultured language.

*

The astute reader will have noticed that the phonic features of poetry and early childhood babble coincide. The conclusion being: while we tend to 'forget' verbal impressions from early childhood, they do resurface in certain abnormal (or rather 'irregular'—lest anyone get scared) states of consciousness, including the poet's state of inspiration; and as they surface, they enter into contact with ordinary language and, owing to their specific characteristics, radically shape the new verbal 'body' that is eventually born of this process—in our case: poetry. The conscious craft of poetry consists precisely in joining and harmonizing infantile and ordinary verbal elements.

And that's how poetry originates in infantile babble.

That's it—for now. If you don't believe me, suit yourself.

Ferdinand de Saussure on the Impossibility of Language Politics

"F. de Saussure o nevozhmosnosti yazykovoy poli-tiki." *Yazykovedenie i materialism* 2 (1931): 91-104. (The majority of the quotes from Saussure's *Cours de linguistique générale* (1916), edited by Charles Bally and Albert Séchehaye, can be found on pages 104-108 of the original.)

> In a certain sense, one can speak both of the immutability and the mutability of the [linguistic] sign.

Charles Bally and Albert Séchehaye, the editors of Saussure's *Course in General Linguistics*, comment on this remark as follows—ironically, destroying its seeming dialectic in the process:

> It would be wrong to accuse Saussure of being illogical or paradoxical in ascribing two mutually contradictory features to language. In juxtaposing these two striking terms (immutability and mutability), he merely wished to underscore the truth that although language transforms itself

61

through time, this transformation cannot be effected by speakers. One could also say that language is inaccessible [intangible] but not in-
alterable [inaltérable].

How interesting: the most prominent represen-
tatives of west European linguistics go out of
their way to 'whitewash' their teacher of the
possible criticism that he ascribes two contra-
dictory qualities to language.

The editors' observation, meanwhile, perfectly captures Saussure's position: he first pro-
poses that it is impossible for speakers to
transform language and then suggests that language does change through time.

In this essay, I will be concerned with the
first proposition.

*

There can be no doubt as to what Saussure
means to say on this subject. He states that "language is entirely dominated by the fact of its historical transmission, which excludes any general
or sudden linguistic changes [exclut tout
changement linguistique général et subit]," and

claims that "the linguistic sign eludes our will [échappe à notre volonté]."

At the very beginning of the chapter entitled "Immutability and Mutability of the Sign," Saussure writes:

If the signifier [le signifiant] appears to have been freely chosen in regard to the idea which it represents, in regard to the linguistic community by which it is employed it is not free at all, it has been imposed. The social mass has never been consulted, the signifier chosen by language itself could not be replaced by another … Not only would an individual—even if he wanted to—be utterly incapable of changing the choice that has been made by language, but the social mass, too, has no power over a single word [ne peut exercer sa souveraineté sur un seul mot]; it is tied to language as it is [liée à la langue telle qu'elle est] … the sign is immutable, which is to say, it resists any arbitrary substitution … In fact, no society has ever known language other than as a product inherited from previous generations to be taken as is [à prendre tel quel].

Saussure's thinking here is crystal-clear: not only does he deny the individual "power over a single word," but he also denies this power to the "social mass," the collective. (In our own domestic linguistic literature these and similar passages in Saussure's *Course* are sometimes interpreted to the effect that Saussure opposes language as a system of arbitrary signs created by the collective to the individual and his individual utterances. As we can see, that's not the case.)

Saussure's view can be summed up as follows: language changes through time as a result of objective conditions, but the subject of language—both the individual speaker and the collective of speakers—does not participate in this process of transformation. The role of the subject of language, who is "tied to language as it is" and cannot step outside the inherited system, is merely passive.

*

Saussure's argument concerning the speakers' powerlessness vis-à-vis language—one of the cornerstones of his entire linguistic system, and closely tied to such other major Saussurean postulates as the "impossibility of a revolution" [l'impossibilité d'une révolution]" in language and the inappropriateness of the question of the origin of language in linguistics—is significant not only as a contribution to theoretical linguistics; it is significant also because, if Saussure is right, then any organized intervention in the linguistic process, any organized societal attempt at impacting the direction of this process, that is, any *language politics* become impossible. (The reason, by the way, that Saussure considers the question of the origin of language inappropriate for linguistics has to do with the fact that for him "the only real object of linguistics is the normal and regular life of a language already constituted.")

Here a purely theoretical, philosophical problem turns (as is only natural) into a problem of general socio-political relevance.

*

To us, the very question "Is language politics possible?" appears misguided. For us, the impossibility of language politics would signify the nugatoriness and methodological impossibility of the very science of language. If Saussure is right, then Marx's sound advice to philosophers—"not only to interpret the world but to change it"—would not be applicable to linguistics. In vain would we "set down the laws" of linguistic evolution if these laws could not be implemented in concrete practice. The question posed to every scientific discipline by our youth—"What is it for?"—is, in its philosophical essence, the most legitimate and necessary of questions. Saussure's response to it is: "For naught"—not, in any case, for changing, transforming, and reorganizing the "inaccessible," concrete reality of our language. The fifteen lines or so that Saussure devotes to the "use of linguistics" at the beginning of his three-hundred-plus-page *Course* are so revealing in this regard that I would like to quote them in full here:

> What, then, is the use of linguistics [l'utilité de la linguistique]? Very few people have a clear idea about this; and this is not the place to try to pin it down. But it is obvious, for example, that linguistic questions interest all those—historians,

philologists, etc.—who deal with texts. Even more obvious is its importance for culture in general [pour la culture générale]: in the life of the individual and in the life of society, language is the most important factor. It would be unacceptable were its study to remain the affair of a handful of specialists; in fact, everybody has a stake in it one way or another [tout le monde s'en occupe peu ou prou]. But—and this is a paradoxical consequence of the very interest that attaches to it: no other area of knowledge has been the breeding ground for so many absurd ideas, prejudices, mirages, and fictions. From a psychological viewpoint, these errors are not negligible; but the linguist's task is, above all, to denounce and debunk them as completely as possible.

Is it necessary for us to prove the possibility of language politics? No. Is it necessary to disprove Saussure's postulate that it is impossible? It is imperative.

*

Saussure's claim that language is inaccessible to its speakers could easily be refuted by simply referring to fact—as aptly captured in Pushkin's famous poem "Motion":

> Motion does not exist—a bearded sage surmised.
> Without a word, another then began to move.
> That's all he had to do the first one wrong to prove
> Receiving praise from all for his astute reply …

*

The history of many "literary" languages offers examples of the transformation of language on the initiative of philologists, literary professionals, etc.

To take a well-known, and fairly typical, case: the redaction from literary Czech of words of German origin (or words suspected of being of German origin), which had far-reaching consequences. As Antoine Meillet notes in *The Languages of the New Europe* (1928):

> The Czech vocabulary has become artificial to a large extent, with derivative and compound words made up of Slavic elements having systematically replaced German words or words resembling the latter. This has isolated Czech not only from all other European language but from

the Slavic languages as well. While Polish has to this day retained many words borrowed from German, which have been organically assimilated and polonized, Czech has only retained the Slavic elements in terms of borrowed linguistic material, and, owing to its exclusively Slavic character, its vocabulary has, in a whole range of instances, no more parallels with Polish, or any other Slavic language. To the point where a widely accepted European word such as *theater*, which is also common in Russian and Polish, has been replaced by *divadlo*, which has no parallels anywhere in Europe.

However, Meillet's examples of the transformation of literary languages may not necessarily be in line with Saussure's approach (even though both are brothers in linguistic spirit), insofar as Saussure considers literary languages artificial in contrast to natural, spoken language:

Any literary language, which is a product of culture, ends up detaching its sphere of existence [arrive à détacher sa sphère d'existence] from the natural sphere, the sphere of spoken language … Is it possible to distinguish the natural, organic development of a language from its artificial forms—such as literary language—which are due to external and, thus, inorganic factors?

(What a muddle! As if spoken language were not a product of culture and did not owe its existence to external factors!)

*

But let's keep in mind the many well-known examples from natural, spoken language that point to the massive significance in this domain of the speakers' conscious and intentional transformation of speech.

These examples could be gleaned from the actual linguistic practices of various social classes. A good number can also be found in the literature dealing with the language of the peasantry (which Saussure would probably consider particularly "natural"). As it turns out, even for the peasant, language reveals itself as far from "inaccessible": the peasant consciously changes his pronunciation, grammar, vocabulary, and phraseology in light of the dictates of metropolitan speech. This conscious departure from the

jouissent les autres institutions]" in terms of their amenability to change through "the free agency of society [l'action libre de la société]." His ensuing train of thought can be boiled down to a complete separation of language from other social institutions and to proving that language cannot be viewed as a model for them, being "entirely dominated by the fact of its historical transmission, which excludes any general or sudden linguistic changes."

*

Saussure adduces four arguments, which he considers the "most essential, the most straight-forward, and on which all others depend." I would like to examine these arguments now. In order to forestall misconstrual and confusion, my own observations on each argument will be preceded by the full text of each of Saussure's four points.

*

1. ——*The arbitrary character of the sign*. Earlier, it forced us to admit the theoretical possibility of change; but digging deeper, we can see that, in

73

fact, the very arbitrariness of the sign shelters language from any attempt at modifying it. The social mass—even it were operating at a much higher level of consciousness than it actually does—would not be capable of discussing language. For an issue to be subjected to interrogation, it must partake of a rational norm. We can, for example, debate the question of whether monogamy is more reasonable than polygamy and adduce reasons for one or the other. We could also discuss a system of symbols, because there is a rational connection between the symbol and the thing symbolized. But in the case of language, which is a system of arbitrary signs, this rational foundation is lacking, and with it any solid ground for discussion as well. There is absolutely no reason to prefer *soeur* to *sister*, *Ochs* to *boeuf*, etc.

Let's agree with Saussure, for the sake of argument, that the linguistic sign is arbitrary, that there is no "rational" connection between the sign's concept—the "signifié"—and its signifying sound combination—the "significant"; that there is no necessity for the concept 'sister' to be represented by the sound combination 'soeur' in French, or for the concept 'bull' to be represented by the sound combination 'Ochs' in German, etc. (I should note, however, that the true nature of the connection between the concept and its corresponding sound combination is completely different from Saussure's description of it, and that it is not at all captured by the formula of the "arbitrariness of the sign." This formula as well as Saussure's theory of the verbal sign as a whole are misguided. The connection between a word and its meaning is historically conditioned, and any attempt at clarifying this connection ultimately leads the question of the origin of language in general and spoken language in particular. Having banned the question of the origin of language from linguistic inquiry, Saussure is obviously incapable of understanding the nature of the word.)

Is it true, though, that discussing the individual linguistic sign and replacing it with another presupposes a "rational" connection between its signifier and its signified? No, it is not. For, its arbitrary character notwithstanding, the linguistic sign does, in fact, get discussed and can be——

and, in fact, is—subject to transformation by speakers.

Meillet extensively deals with the question as to which sound combination (significant) is more "suitable" for the concept (signifié) 'theater' in Czech; he reaches the conclusion that it is definitely not 'divadlo'—the contemporary Czech word for 'theater'. Much more suitable would be the sound combination that corresponds to the German 'Theater', the French 'téâtre', the English 'theatre', the Russian 'teatr', etc. As it turns out, the word 'divadlo' was *chosen* by the Czech to replace the Czech word that morphologically corresponded to the Russian 'teatr', etc., as a result of elaborate "discussion."

Isn't the question as to which signifier is more "suitable" for the Russian concept 'techyet' [flows/is flowing]—'techyet' or 'tekyet'—amenable to discussion, and isn't it, in fact, being discussed? Isn't it possible and not at all unnecessary to discuss and decide on what's better in Russian: 'ikh' or 'ikhny' (variants of the possessive pronoun their[s]), 'mólodezh' or 'molodyézh' (variants of 'youth'), 'mestov' or 'mest' (variants of the genitive form of 'places': 'of places' or 'places''). Don't we have idiosyncratic debates about and decisions on our own local idioms whenever the speakers of any given dialect or local idiom begin to depart from the latter and adapt to more widely accepted speech and pronunciation. It is true that in such cases we certainly don't have discussions in print or at public gatherings with arguments presented and votes cast, but Saussure doesn't necessarily have this type of public discussion in mind to begin with.

*

Saussure could not have been ignorant of facts analogous to the ones I have provided. Why, then, didn't he take them into account? (Did he simply forget or intentionally ignore them?) Clearly, in doing so, he was merely living up to the standards of his own abstract formal-logical thinking: in positing the arbitrariness of the linguistic sign, and claiming from this abstract formal-logical vantage point that there is no good reason to prefer the French 'boeuf' to the German 'Ochs', Saussure completely lost sight of the fact that just as real bulls the words designating them do not exist somewhere between heaven and earth, cut off from the rest of the world. Saussure does not consider the linguistic sign in its relation to other things and phenomena; he does not take into account that in existing within the dynamic system of evolving language, the linguistic sign enters into a plethora of rational and irrational relations—both linguistic and non-linguistic—and is very much subject to discussion and debate. Saussure does not take into account the inherent contradictoriness of the linguistic sign: it is arbitrary, fortuitous, and neutral if considered in light of its discrete internal structure; but it is anything but arbitrary, fortuitous, and neutral in its emplacement in the dynamism of the ever-evolving system of language and society as a whole.

The peasant transforms his system of linguistic signs in conjunction with the transformation of technology, his way of life and thinking, striving to attain the standards of the next higher social class or group. Similarly, at some point, the

Czech bourgeoisie began using the word 'divadlo' to refer to 'theater' because it was struggling against its Germanized feudal lords. And the Russian 'techyet' is preferable to 'tekyet' because it is a better grammatical fit within the overall system of the Russian language; or, some might say, it is better because that's how educated, cultured people speak and great writers write. And perhaps for someone the French bull might be preferable to the German bull because his wife happens to be French.

But all jokes aside, it is blatantly evident that there may be a plethora of reasons to prefer one signifier to another. Certainly, not all reasons will be instrumental in contributing to the transformation of language; but the very dynamic of its practical existence renders language inseparable from its concrete historical content, which, in turn, reveals the linguistic sign as anything but neutral to the speakers and very much the subject of possible "discussion." (Which yet again underscores how mistaken Saussure is in suggesting that "linguistic facts do not in any way elicit criticism" and that "each people tends to be satisfied with the language it has received.")

*

2. ——*The multitude of signs necessary for the constitution any language.* The consequences of this fact are considerable. A system of writing made up of twenty to forty letters could, if need be, be replaced by another. The same would apply to language if it were made up of a limited number of elements; but the linguistic signs are infinite.

Let me first note that this point squarely contradicts the previous one. Here, Saussure actually admits the possibility of transforming, and even replacing, a system of written sings; that is, he suggests that the written sign is not at all inaccessible to the "social mass." It being obvious, though, that the internal structure of the written linguistic sign is the same as the internal structure of the spoken (phonic) linguistic sign——insofar as in the written linguistic sign, too, the connection between signifier and signified is arbitrary——and given that, according to Saussure himself, systems of arbitrary signs are subject to transformation by their users after all, this means that the entire previous argument concerning the impossibility of the intentional linguistic transformation of language by its speakers owing to the arbitrariness of the sign crumbles before our very eyes.

If we consider the second point on its own merits, then the argument appears to rest on the distinction between the presumed potential infinity of spoken signs as opposed to the limited number of written signs, whereby it is precisely the potential infinity of spoken signs that presumably makes the transformation of language by its speakers impossible.

It's not at all clear, however, how the alleged infinity of (spoken) linguistic signs bears on the question of the mutability or immutability of language in the first place, and why it should make a *partial* transformation of language by its speakers impossible, for instance? Keeping in mind that it has never been a question of replacing an entire linguistic system by another, but merely of the possibility of *transforming* a linguistic system, of its *accessibility* to its speakers.

Furthermore, Saussure is completely wrong in opposing spoken to written language based on the difference in the number of signs each allegedly has—infinite and limited, respectively. As far as the number aspect is concerned, both systems are categorically identical. If, in speaking of an infinite number of signs, Saussure actually had individual speech ("parole") in mind, one might agree with him—barely, though, since in written language, too, the individual written utterance implies an infinite number of signs (including the writer's singular hand, etc.). But Saussure cannot possibly mean "parole" here (if he did he would stop being Saussure); what he must mean here is not "parole" but language as a system—"langue." And can the number of signs in "langue" *qua* system of linguistic signs be infinite? Of course not! For can't we say that the actual system of language consists of twenty to forty sounds, in analogy with Saussure's observation that the system of written language consists of twenty to forty letters? How can the number of grammatical signs be infinite? And if Saussure means the infinite number of words in spoken language, then the number of words in written language must also be infinite—but in this case, too, there's no point in speaking of infinity.

Chasing arguments, Saussure ascribes qualities to language that language does not possess and tries to fob us off with muddled hyperboles instead offering compelling proofs.

*

3. ——*The overly complex character of the system.* A language constitutes a system. If, as we shall see, this is the aspect on account of which it is not completely arbitrary [n'est pas complètement arbitraire] and governed by reason—relatively speaking [il règne une raison relative]—it is also the aspect that reveals the inability [l'incompétence] of the mass to transform it. For this system is a complex mechanism; it can only be grasped through reflection [réflexion]; even those who use it daily are profoundly ignorant [l'ignorent profondément] in its regard. One couldn't conceive of such transformation other than effected by specialists, grammarians, logicians, etc. But experience shows that such attempts have, thus far, had absolutely no success.

(Interestingly, remembering that language is a system, Saussure disavows, if cautiously, its complete arbitrariness. Unfortunately, he didn't remember this when making the first of his four cardinal claims, which would have—had he remembered it—wilted before its prime.)

Two moments need to be distinguished in Saussure's third point: 1. the impossibility of transforming language by the "mass"; 2. the impossibility (or improbability) of such transformation by specialists as well.

The "mass" cannot transform language because it is "profoundly ignorant" of its "complex mechanism" and can never know it. Why? Because the common man, Saussure implies, does not engage in "reflection" on language. Saussure's mistake consists in assuming that knowledge necessarily implies contemplation and reflection. Certainly, the "mass" is not made up of academics and philologists who contemplate language, thereby cognizing its "complex mechanism." But the "mass" may very well 'cognize'—if not exhaustively—the "complex mechanism" of language in action: for it is the "mass" that concretely *realizes* language.

It is crucial to note that the coexistence of diverse language systems, or rather, the coexistence of collectives with different language systems, greatly facilitates opening up the complexities of these systems to their speakers and, thus, also to their transformation by them.

As far as the impossibility of linguistic transformation by specialists is concerned—i. e., the impossibility of *language politics* in the true sense of the term—Saussure's only 'proof' consists in pointing out that any "such attempts" have so far been unsuccessful (as experience shows!). Leaving aside the question whether "such attempts" have or have not been successful, by the same token it could have been argued in the past that reaching the north pole or flying in apparatuses heavier than air would remain impossible, etc. (Of course, "such attempts" have been successful in a number of cases.)

For his reliance on experience to be more than fatuous and anecdotal, Saussure would need to show that the conditions under which the experience referred to has been gained will always remain the same—something he neither does nor even considers, viewing the once-established social situation as a static given.

*

4. —*The resistance of collective inertia to all linguistic innovation.* Language is—and this aspect trumps all others—the business of all, all the time [à chaque moment l'affaire de tout le monde]. Spread across a mass and handled by it, it is something everybody uses all day long. In this respect, it cannot be compared with any other institution. The prescriptions of a code, the rites of a religion, maritime signals, etc. never concern more than a certain number of individuals at a time [à la fois], and for limited periods. Language, by contrast, is something everybody takes part in all the time, and that is why it is constantly subject to the influence of all. This cardinal fact suffices to prove the impossibility of a revolution [l'impossibilité d'une revolution] in language. Of all the social institutions, language is the one that offers the least openings for initiatives. It constitutes a single whole with the

life of the social mass, and the latter, being naturally inert [étant naturellement inerte], appears, above all, as a force of conservation.

Saussure's first observation is: language is the business of all; it constitutes a single whole with the life of the "social mass"; everybody takes part in language all the time.

Saussure's second observation is: the "social mass" is naturally inert and reveals itself, above all, as a force of conservation.

The conclusion being … but there's no point in speaking of a conclusion here, given that the second observation is obviously completely wrong. Ascribing inertia to the "social mass" as though it were an immutable quality means understanding nothing about the dialectical process of social evolution. The mythical "mass" constantly invoked by Saussure is neither monolithic nor undifferentiated—far from it: it is divided into classes, whose "activity" and "inertia" vis-à-vis possible "initiatives," including those in the domain of language, vary greatly at any given point in time.

Thus, at the beginning of the nineteenth century the Czech bourgeoisie was so *not* inert that the "initiatives" of "specialists" to transform the Czech language were widely able to take hold and generate lasting results.

Insofar as Saussure's claim concerning the inertia of the "social mass" is misguided, his concomitant claim that "language is the business of all, all the time" reveals itself as meaningless. In fact, the latter appears to undermine Saussure's very argument here: for the fact that language is the business of all makes its transformation in any given situation all the more possible. This, then, is the sorry state of Saussure's fourth—and most important—point in his overall argument.

*

Thus, neither the arbitrariness of the linguistic sign, nor the number of signs necessary to constitute any language, nor the overly complex character of the system, nor, finally, the opposition of social inertia to any form of linguistic innovation prove in any way that language is "inaccessible" to its speakers. Far from it: language is very much accessible to its speakers and does, in fact, get transformed by them. Saussure's attempt to prove the impossibility of language politics fails.

*

What are the methodological roots of Saussure's failure and what is its sociological equivalent? Why did Saussure go wrong?

Because he approaches his object formally-logically, without considering the skein of concrete social relations in which it actually exists.

Because he thinks that language can only be known through reflection, contemplation from the sidelines, so to speak, all the while forgetting about the subject of language, the collective.

Because in taking account neither of the class divisions in society nor of the dialectical process of social and linguistic evolution, he views the social structure as a whole in squarely abstract, ahistorical terms, ascribing qualities to the mass of speakers as a whole that only apply to some of its parts, to this or that social class at a particular moment in its historical evolution.

Name Index

- Pushkin, Aleksandr Sergeyevich (1799-1837), Russian poet
- Séchehaye, Albert (1870-1946), Swiss linguist
- Tolstoy, Aleksey Konstantinovich (1817-1875), Russian novelist
- Turgenev, Ivan Sergeyevich (1818-1883), Russian novelist
- Vyazemsky, Prince Pyotr Andreyevich (1792-1878), Russian poet
- Wundt, Wilhelm (1832-1920), German physician, physiologist and philosopher
- Zelinsky, Tadeusz Stefan (1859-1944), Polish-Russian philologist

Available from UWSP

- *November Rose: A Speech on Death*
  by Kathrin Stengel (2008 Independent
  Publisher Book Award)

- *November-Rose: Eine Rede über den Tod*
  by Kathrin Stengel

- *Philosophical Fragments of a Contemporary Life*
  by Julien David

- *17 Vorurteile, die wir Deutschen gegen Amerika
  und die Amerikaner haben und die so nicht ganz
  stimmen können* by Misha Waiman

- *The DNA of Prejudice: On the One and the Many*
  by Michael Eskin (2010 Next Generation
  Indie Book Award for Social Change)

- *Descartes' Devil: Three Meditations*
  by Durs Grünbein

- *Fatal Numbers: Why Count on Chance*
  by Hans Magnus Enzensberger
- *The Vocation of Poetry* by Durs Grünbein
  (2011 Independent Publisher Book Award)

- *The Waiting Game: An Essay on the Gift of Time*
  by Andrea Köhler (out of print)

- *Mortal Diamond: Poems* by Durs Grünbein

- *Yoga for the Mind: A New Ethic for Thinking and Being & Meridians of Thought* by Michael Eskin & Kathrin Stengel (2014 Living Now Book Award)

- *The Wisdom of Parenthood: An Essay* by Michael Eskin

- *Health is in Your Hands: Jin Shin Jyutsu — Practicing the Art of Self-Healing (With 51 Flash Cards for the Hands-On Practice of Jin Shin Jyutsu)* by Waltraud Riegger-Krause (2015 Living Now Book Award for Healing Arts)

- *A Moment More Sublime: A Novel* by Stephen Grant

- *High on Low: Harnessing the Power of Unhappiness* by Wilhelm Schmid (2015 Living Now Book Award for Personal Growth)

- *Become a Message: Poems* by Lajos Walder (2016 Benjamin Franklin Award)

- *What We Gain As We Grow Older: On Gelassenheit* by Wilhelm Schmid (2016 Living Now Gold Award)

- *On Dialogic Speech* by L. P. Yakubinsky

- *Tyrtaeus: A Tragedy* by Lajos Walder

- *Vase of Pompeii: A Play* by Lajos Walder

- *Below Zero: A Play* by Lajos Walder

- *Passing Time: An Essay on Waiting* by Andrea Köhler

- *In Praise of Weakness* by Alexandre Jollien

- *Homo Conscius: A Novel* by Timothy Balding

- *Spanish Light: A Novel* by Stephen Grant

- *On Language & Poetry* by L. P. Yakubinsky

- *Potentially Harmless: A Philosopher's Manhattan*
  by Kathrin Stengel (forthcoming)

Designed by UWSP

Printed in the United States of America